Jim Henson
Creator of the Muppets

by Rita Petrucelli

illustrated by Luciano Lazzarino

Rourke Enterprises Vero Beach, Florida

Manufactured in the United States of America

Library of Congress Cataloging-in-Publication Data

Petrucelli, Rita, 1942-
 Jim Henson, creator of the Muppets / Rita Petrucelli.
  p. cm. —(Reaching your goal)
 Summary: A biography of the puppeteer whose remark-
able creations, the Muppets, have found success in television and other media. Includes advice on setting and
reaching goals.
 1. Henson, Jim—Juvenile literature. 2. Puppeteers—
United States—Biography—Juvenile literature. [1. Henson,
Jim. 2. Puppeteers. 3. Television producers and directors.
4. Muppet show (Television program)] I. Title. II. Series:
Martin, Patricia Stone. Reaching your goal.
PN1982.H46P48   1989
791.5'3'0924—dc19
[B]   88-11602
[92]   CIP
ISBN 0-86592-426-0   AC

The moving van pulled up in front of Jim Henson's house. The Hensons were leaving Greenville, Mississippi. They were moving to Maryland. Moving away was hard for Jim. He would miss his friends. Jim was born in Greenville and had lived there all his life. He was thirteen years old. Jim was a very shy boy. He wondered if making new friends would be hard.

Jim's family settled into their new home. They even bought a TV set. TVs were new then. Not too many people had them.

Jim liked watching TV. His favorite program was the "Kukla, Fran and Ollie" show. Kukla was a puppet. So was Ollie, the dragon. Fran was a real person. She talked with the puppets. Fran and the puppets made Jim laugh.

4

Jim joined a puppet club in high school. There he practiced making puppets. Jim was a good artist. He drew pictures of puppets. Then he built the puppets to look like the pictures.

Before Jim went off to college, he tried out for a local TV show. In his act, Jim used the puppets he had made. Jim got the job. The show lasted only three weeks though. That didn't stop Jim. He was on his way to becoming a very famous puppeteer.

Jim worked hard in college. He studied acting and art. He also learned how to design stage sets. Jim and his puppets appeared on more local TV shows. Jim operated the puppets. He used different voices to speak for them. Important people began to notice Jim Henson's work, and they liked it very much.

In 1955 something special happened to Jim. He had an offer to do his own TV show. The show would be seen very late at night. It would be on for only five minutes. That was good enough for Jim and his puppets. The show was called "Sam and Friends."

Jim needed someone to help him operate the puppets on the show. He asked his friend Jane Nebel. Jane was a student at the same college. She was also interested in puppets.

Jim and Jane became a team. They made TV commercials using puppets they had created. The commercials were very good. A TV station owner in New York City watched the commercials. He invited Jim to New York City. He wanted Jim and Jane to do their puppet act on the "Tonight Show."

People all across the U.S. saw Jim Henson's puppets. The puppet act starred a frog named Kermit. Kermit wore a blond wig. He sang the song "I've Grown Accustomed to Your Face" to a purple monster. The monster ate its own face! Then it tried to eat Kermit! The audience laughed. The puppets were a big hit.

A few years later, a new TV show was being made for children. The name of the show was "Sesame Street." Puppets would be used to help teach children about reading and math. Jim Henson was asked to created those puppets. So Jim created the Cookie Monster, Oscar the Grouch, Animal, and many other puppets. Kermit and Miss Piggy appeared on the show too.

Jim called his puppets "Muppets." Why? Because of the way he operated them. To work a hand puppet, Jim's hand moved inside the puppet's head. The Muppets were more than hand puppets though. Jim moved their bodies too. He moved different parts of the puppets' bodies with strings — like he would move a marionette. Jim took the *M* from marionette and the *uppets* from puppets. It came out *Muppets!*

"Sesame Street" was a big hit. It won a special award. The award was for the best children's program. The award made Jim both happy and unhappy. Jim's goal was to make the Muppets fun for everyone, not just children.

Jim tried to sell his idea of a family Muppet show to three TV station owners. None of them were interested.

A man named Lord Grade heard about Jim's Muppets. Lord Grade lived in England. England is a country far across the ocean from the U.S. Lord Grade invited Jim to produce the "Muppet Show" there. Jim packed up his Muppets and went to England. Each week he produced a new show. Millions of people around the world watched the "Muppet Show."

At the end of one year, the "Muppet Show" won an award for the best show of the year. This time the award wasn't for the best children's show. Jim Henson proved that his Muppets were fun for children and grown ups. He had reached his goal. But Jim didn't stop there. He set new goals for himself. Jim was a hard worker.

"Many people think of work as something to avoid," says Jim. "I think of work as something to seek."

Meet the Fraggles!

Kermit, Miss Piggy, and all the Muppets became famous TV stars. Jim wanted to make them movie stars too. So Jim produced a feature film called *The Muppet Movie*. A few years later two more movies, *The Great Muppet Caper* and *The Muppets Take Manhattan,* were shown in theaters all around the world.

Later, Jim produced two more movies, *The Dark Crystal* and *Labyrinth*. He also created a new children's TV show called "Fraggle Rock." These movies and the TV show didn't star the famous Muppets. Jim created all new Muppets.

Today Jim Henson has a big workshop in
New York City. Many people work for Jim
there. Some people create new Muppets.
Others learn how to operate them.

"It all starts with a sketch," says Jim. "Then
we begin building a Muppet."

It can take a week to build the hands of
one Muppet. Each Muppet has a personality
too. For example, Kermit is a little shy. Miss
Piggy has her snout into everything. Oscar is
a grouch. And Animal is wild!

Learning how to be one of Jim's puppeteers takes about two years. Puppeteers stand beneath the stage. Sometimes, two puppeteers are needed to work the head, hands, and body parts of one Muppet.

People like working for Jim Henson. "Everything about him is special," says Amy, one of his Muppet makers. "He brings out the best in everyone," says another worker.

More than 30 years have passed since Jim Henson first appeared on TV. In that time, Jim created the Muppets. He made several movies and TV shows. He even married his puppet partner, Jane Nebel.

Today, Jim and Jane have five children. Jim spends a great deal of time running his business. He is still shy and quiet. When Jim works away from home on a movie, he likes to have fun. How does Jim have fun? He skateboards or flies kites with his workers.

Jim Henson has made the Muppets famous around the world. He has brought fun and laughter to many children and grown ups. Jim began working with puppets just for fun. He turned puppet fun into a big business.

Jim has reached many goals during his lifetime. Even so, he has at least one more goal. What's that? Jim hopes that his TV shows and movies will teach children how to be good people. He hopes children will learn how to work well together.

21

Reaching Your Goal

What are your goals? Here are some steps to help you reach them.

1. **Decide on your goal.**
   It may be a short-term goal like one of these:
   learning to ride a bike
   getting a good grade on a test
   keeping your room clean
   It may be a long-term goal like one of these:
   learning to read
   learning to play the piano
   becoming a lawyer

2. **Decide if your goal is something you really can do.**
   Do you have the talent you need?
   How can you find out? By trying!
   Will you need special equipment?
   Perhaps you need a piano or ice skates.
   How can you get what you need?
   Ask your teacher or your parents.

22

3. Decide on the first thing you must do.
   Perhaps this will be to take lessons.

4. Decide on the second thing you must do.
   Perhaps this will be to practice every day.

5. Start right away.
   Stick to your plan until you reach your goal.

6. Keep telling yourself, "I can do it!"

Good Luck! Maybe some day you will become a puppeteer like Jim Henson!

Reaching Your Goal Books

Beverly Cleary She Makes Reading Fun

Bill Cosby Superstar

Jesse Jackson A Rainbow Leader

Ted Kennedy, Jr. A Lifetime of Challenges

Christa McAuliffe Reaching for the Stars

Dale Murphy Baseball's Gentle Giant

Dr. Seuss We Love You

Samantha Smith Young Ambassador

Michael Jordan A Team Player

Steven Spielberg He Makes Great Movies

Charles Schulz Great Cartoonist

Cher Singer and Actress

Ray Kroc McDonald's Man

Hans Christian Andersen A Fairy Tale Life

Henry Cisneros A Hard Working Mayor

Jim Henson Creator of the Muppets

Rourke Enterprises, Inc.
P.O. Box 3328
Vero Beach, FL 32964

B
HEN

Petrucelli, Rita.

Jim Henson, creator
of the Muppets.

$8.00

B
HEN

Petrucelli, Rita.

Jim Henson, creator
of the Muppets.